As a Man Thinketh

Annotated Integration Edition

By: James Allen

With commentary and exercises by:
Sufijan Cunningham

"As A Man Thinketh" written by James Allen was first published in 1890 by James Pott and Co. Philadelphia.

The original Text is now in public domain

2017 Feeling The Flow Publishing

Introduction

This has been one of my favorite books since I first read it. For some of you, this will be an amazing refresher of things you have heard before, for others it will be a brand new experience.

I decided to create this workbook to help the information sink in. Sometimes when we read things we don't quite find the bridge to relate the information to our own life. I have added my own commentary in this same font you are reading to give some needed pauses and get you to re-engage a different part of your brain while reading. Each section also has a question and answer exercise. The practice of writing out your answers will help you gain mastery over this amazing work.

Keep in mind, this book was written in 1890 and throughout the book James Allen refers to "man" as opposed to man and woman. This was a common way of writing back then. Rest assured this book is relevant to all and if he says man, know he is talking about mankind or humankind as a whole.

The book is presented with infinite gratitude to James Allen himself. Without his decision to direct his creative faculties we wouldn't have this book. I am also grateful to all who have published and shared this book over the last 100 years to get it into my hands so many years later.

I hope this book benefits you even 1/2 as much as it did me.

-Sufijan

Forward

This little volume (the result of meditation and experience) is not intended as an exhaustive treatise on the much-written-upon subject of the power of thought. It is suggestive rather than explanatory, its object being to stimulate men and women to the discovery and perception of the truth that "They themselves are makers of themselves" by virtue of the thoughts which they choose and encourage; that mind is the master weaver, both of the inner garment of character and the outer garment of circumstance, and that, as they may have hitherto woven in ignorance and pain they may now weave in enlightenment and happiness.

James Allen Ilfracombe, England

Thought And Character

"As a man thinketh in his heart, so is he," not only embraces the whole of a man's being, but is so comprehensive as to reach out to every condition and circumstance of his life. A man is literally what he thinks, his character being the complete sum of all his thoughts.

As the plant springs from, and could not be without, the seed, so every act of man springs from the hidden seeds of thought, and could not have appeared without them. This applies equally to those acts called "spontaneous" and "unpremeditated" as to those which are deliberately executed.

Act is the blossom of thought, and joy and suffering are its fruit; thus does a man garner in the sweet and bitter fruitage of his own husbandry.

Thought in the mind hath made us. What we are by thought was wrought and built. If a man's mind hath evil thought, pain comes on him as comes the wheel the ox behind. If one endure in purity of thought, Joy follows him as his own shadow - sure.

Man is a growth by law, and not a creation by artifice, and cause and effect are as absolute and undeviating in the hidden realm of thought as in the world of visible and material things. A noble and God-like character is not a thing of favor or chance, but is the natural result of continued effort in right thinking, the effect of long-cherished association with God-like thoughts. An ignoble and bestial character, by the same process, is the result of the continued harboring of groveling thoughts.

> <u>Contemplation</u>:
> We've all heard the phrase "You are what you eat", the new version is "You are what you think about"!

Man is made or unmade by himself. In the armory of thought he forges the weapons by which he destroys himself. He also fashions the tools with which he builds for himself heavenly mansions of joy and strength and peace. By the right choice and true application of thought, man ascends to the divine perfection. By the abuse and wrong application of thought he descends below the level of the beast. Between these two extremes are all the grades of character, and man is their maker and master.

<u>Contemplation</u>:

What he's really saying here is that you must take Self Responsibility. There's no outside force to blame, you and only you are in charge. At first this may seem scary, taking on responsibility often does, but once you realize that it simply means you're in control, then you feel the freedom!

Of all the beautiful truths pertaining to the soul which have been restored and brought to light in this age, none is more gladdening or fruitful of divine promise and confidence than this-- that man is the master of thought, the molder of character, and the maker and shaper of condition, environment, and destiny.

As a being of power, intelligence, and love, and the lord of his own thoughts, man holds the key to every situation, and contains within himself that transforming and regenerative agency by which he may make himself what he wills.

Man is always the master, even in his weakest and most abandoned state. But in his weakness and degradation he is foolish master who misgoverns his "household." When he begins to reflect upon his condition and search diligently for the law upon which his being is established, he then becomes the wise master, directing his energies with intelligence and fashioning his thoughts to fruitful issues. Such is the conscious master, and man can only thus become by discovering within himself the laws of thought. This discovery is totally a matter of application, self-analysis and experience.

> **The Work:**
>
> It takes time, practice and patience to become a master of one's thoughts. We're often used to being led by our thoughts, being a follower. Taking back control puts you in a position of leadership. This takes time to cultivate.

Only by much searching and mining are gold and diamonds obtained, and man can find every truth connected with his being, if he will dig deep into the mine of his soul. That he is the maker of his character, the molder of his life, and the builder of his destiny, he may unerringly prove, if he will watch, control, and alter his thoughts, tracing their effects upon himself, upon others and upon his life and circumstances, linking cause and effect by patient practice and investigation. And utilizing his every experience, even the most trivial, everyday occurrence, as a means of obtaining that knowledge of himself which is understanding, wisdom, power. In this direction, as in no other, is the law absolute that "He that seeketh findeth; and to him that knocketh it shall be opened." For only by patience, practice, and ceaseless importunity can a man enter the door of the temple of knowledge.

> **The Work:**
>
> There is a concept that helps out when starting this kind of thought master. It's called the 4 stages of learning. It looks like this:

Stage 4:
Unconsciously
Competent

Stage 3:
Consciously
Competent

Stage 2:
Consciously
Incompetent

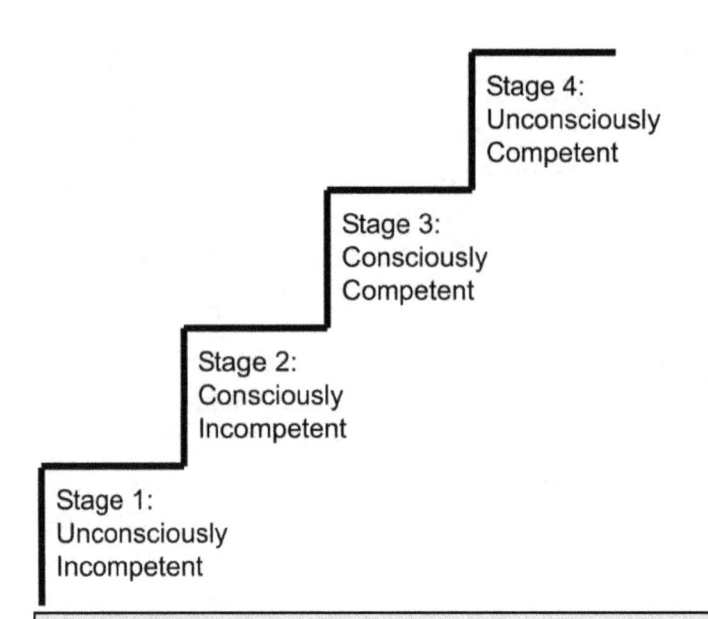

Stage 1:
Unconsciously
Incompetent

You start at the bottom, the phrase "You don't know what you don't know" describes Stage 1 perfectly. As a baby your parents put your shoes on and you didn't even see them, you didn't know they had shoelaces, you didn't really even know what a shoelace was. Then you step up to Stage 2, at some point as a small child you realized you had feet, that wore shoes, held on by laces, that you didn't know how to tie. You became conscious of your own incompetence. You now "know what you don't know". Next at Stage 3, you are taught how to tie a shoe, it's hard and you don't always get it right, you have to remember which side you start with and which one is the loop and what wraps around. You mess up sometimes, but you slowly get better. Finally you get to stage 4, you know how to tie a shoe so well that you don't even think about it, you have total muscle memory and tie a perfect knot every time.

You will need to go through these stages as you take leadership over your thoughts and mind, be patient with yourself and know that you're learning. You're not yet at the mastery level, Stage 4, but you will get there.

Exercises:

What are some examples in my life of moving through these 4 stages. How long did it take?

What did I learn?

What helped me move from one stage to the next?

_____
_____
_____
_____
_____
_____
_____
_____
_____
_____
_____
_____
_____
_____
_____
_____
_____
_____
_____
_____
_____
_____

What new thoughts will I need to create to build the life of my dreams?

Effect Of Thought On Circumstances

A man's mind may be likened to a garden, which may be intelligently cultivated or allowed to run wild; but whether cultivated or neglected, it must, and will bring forth. If no useful seeds are put into it, then an abundance of useless weed-seeds will fall therein, and will continue to produce their kind.

Just as a gardener cultivates his plot, keeping it free from weeds, and growing the flowers and fruits which he requires so may a man tend the garden of his mind, weeding out all the wrong, useless and impure thoughts, and cultivating toward perfection the flowers and fruits of right, useful and pure thoughts. By pursuing this process, a man sooner or later discovers that he is the master-gardener of his soul, the director of his life. He also reveals, within himself, the flaws of thought, and understands, with ever-increasing accuracy, how the thought-forces and mind elements operate in the shaping of character, circumstances, and destiny.

Thought and character are one, and as character can only manifest and discover itself through environment and circumstance, the outer conditions of a person's life will always be found to be harmoniously related to his inner state. This does not mean that a man's circumstances at any given time are an indication of his entire character, but that those circumstances are so intimately connected with some vital thought-element within himself that, for the time being, they are indispensable to his development.

Every man is where he is by the law of his being; the thoughts which he has built into his character have brought him there, and in the arrangement of his life there is no element of chance, but all is the result of a law which cannot err. This is just as true of those who feel "out of harmony" with their surroundings as of those who are contented with them.

> Contemplation:
>
> Character is the result of one's actions and actions are the result of your thoughts. Character is often how others view us. People often feel that others can't read their mind, but if one can see your actions and character then they know the thoughts that came before! Character is the impression we leave on the world.
>
> I'm sure you've had an experience meeting someone for the first time and there was an immediate reaction, good, bad, or neutral. This came from you ability to immediately judge the character and "read their mind or thoughts". The good news is that you control how other see you by adjusting your thoughts and actions.

As a progressive and evolving being, man is where he is that he may learn that he may grow; and as he learns the spiritual lesson which any circumstance contains for him, it passes away and gives place to other circumstances.

Man is buffeted by circumstances so long as he believes himself to be the creature of outside conditions, but when he realizes that he is a creative power, and that he may command the hidden soil and seeds of his being out of which circumstances grow; he then becomes the rightful master of himself.

> The Work:
>
> Don't get held back by the past, what you thought, did, or what you allowed to happen to you. Simply acknowledge it, label it as I like that and want more, or I don't like that and I choose to eliminate. Then proceed with that awareness and create from the present moment.

That circumstances grow out of thought every man knows who has for any length of time practiced self-control and self-purification, for he will have noticed that the alteration in his circumstances has been in exact ratio with his altered mental condition. So true is this that when a man earnestly applies himself to remedy the defects in his character, and makes swift and marked progress, he passes rapidly through a succession of vicissitudes.

The soul attracts that which it secretly harbors, that which it loves, and also that which it fears. It reaches the height of its cherished aspirations; it falls to the level of its unchastened desires, and circumstances are the means by which the soul receives it own. Every thought-seed sown or allowed to fall into the mind, and to take root there, produces its own, blossoming sooner or later into act, and bearing its own fruitage of opportunity and circumstance. Good thoughts bear good fruit, bad thoughts bad fruit.

The outer world of circumstances shapes itself to the inner world of thought, and both pleasant and unpleasant external conditions are factors which make for the ultimate good of the individual. As the reaper of his own harvest, man learns both of suffering and bliss.

Following the inmost desires, aspirations, thoughts, by which he allows himself to be dominated (pursuing the will-o'-the wisps of impure imaginings or steadfastly walking the highway of strong and high endeavor), a man at last arrives at their fruition and fulfillment in the outer conditions of his life.

The laws of growth and adjustment everywhere obtain. A man does not come to the alms-house or the jail by the tyranny of fate or circumstance, but by the pathway of groveling thoughts and base desires. Nor does a pure-minded man fall suddenly into crime by stress of any mere external force. The criminal thought had long been secretly fostered in the heart, and the hour of opportunity revealed its gathered power. Circumstance does not make the man;

it reveals him to himself.

No such conditions can exist as descending into vice and its attendant sufferings apart from vicious inclinations, or ascending into virtue and its pure happiness without the continued cultivation of virtuous aspirations; and man, therefore, as the lord and master of thought, is the maker of himself and the shaper of and author of environment. Even at birth the soul comes of its own and through every step of its earthly pilgrimage it attracts those combinations of conditions which reveal itself, which are the reflections of its own purity and impurity, its strength and weakness.

Men do not attract that which they want, but that which they are. Their whims, fancies, and ambitions are thwarted at every step, but their inmost thoughts and desires are fed with their own food, be it foul or clean. Man is manacled only by himself; thought and action are the jailers of Fate--they imprison, being base; they are also the angels of Freedom--they liberate, being noble.

> <u>Contemplation</u>:
>
> We are only fated as much as we think we are. The only fate we have is to be in complete control and have the will to exert our power over our lives. This law is already at work in your life whether you know it or not. It's what has brought you everything in your life up to this point and will continue delivering a reflection back to you. Change your internal pattern and you'll be met with a harmonic world on the outside as well.

Not what he wished and prays for does a man get, but what he justly earns. His wishes and prayers are only gratified and answered when they harmonize with his thoughts and actions.

In the light of this truth what, then, is the meaning of "fighting against circumstances?" It means that a man is continually revolting against an effect without, while all the time he is nourishing and preserving its cause in his heart.

> **Reflection:**
> We all know people who are all talk and no action. We have all been that person at one point or another in the past. Our actions speak so loudly they drown out everything we say.

That cause may take the form of a conscious vice or an unconscious weakness; but whatever it is, it stubbornly retards the efforts of it possessor, and thus calls aloud for remedy.

Men are anxious to improve their circumstances, but are unwilling to improve themselves; they therefore remain bound. The man who does not shrink from self-crucifixion can never fail to accomplish the object upon which his heart is set. This is as true of earthly as of heavenly things. Even the man whose sole object is to acquire wealth must be prepared to make great personal sacrifices before he can accomplish his object; and how much more so he who would realize a strong and well-poised life?

> **Contemplation:**
> There is a certain level of perceived sacrifice. Although what you'll realize is that the things you "sacrificed" in order to become who you choose to be where things you really didn't need anyway!

Here is a man who is wretchedly poor. He is extremely anxious that his surroundings and home comforts should improve, yet all the time he shirks his work, and considers he is justified in trying to deceive his employer on the ground of the insufficiency of his wages. Such a man does not understand the simplest rudiments of those principles which are the basis of true prosperity, and is not only totally unfitted to rise out of his wretchedness, but is actually attracting to himself a still deeper wretchedness by dwelling in, and acting out, indolent, deceptive, and unmanly thoughts.

Here is a rich man who is the victim of a painful and persistent disease as the result of gluttony. He is willing to give large sums of money to get rid of it, but he will not sacrifice his gluttonous desires. He wants to gratify his taste for rich and unnatural foods and have his health as well. Such a man is totally unfit to have health, because he has not yet learned the first principles of a healthy life.

Here is an employer of labor who adopts crooked measures to avoid paying the regulation wage, and, in the hope of making larger profits, reduces the wages of his workpeople. Such a man is altogether unfitted for prosperity. And when he finds himself bankrupt, both as regards reputation and riches, he blames circumstances, not knowing that he is the sole author of his condition.

I have introduced these three cases merely as illustrative of the truth that man is the causer (though nearly always unconsciously) of his circumstances, and that, whilst aiming at the good end, he is continually frustrating its accomplishment by encouraging thoughts and desires which cannot possibly harmonize with that end. Such cases could be multiplied and varied almost indefinitely, but this is not necessary. The reader can, if he so resolves, trace the action of the laws of thought in his own mind and life, and until this is done, mere external facts cannot serve as a ground of reasoning.

Circumstances, however, are so complicated, thought is so deeply rooted, and the conditions of happiness vary so vastly with individuals, that a man's entire soul condition (although it may be known to himself) cannot be judged by another from the external aspect of his life alone.

A man may be honest in certain directions, yet suffer privations. A man may be dishonest in certain directions, yet acquire wealth. But the conclusion usually formed that the one man fails because of his particular honesty, and that the other prospers because of his particular dishonesty, is the result of a superficial judgment, which assumes that the dishonest man is almost totally corrupt, and honest man almost entirely virtuous. In the light of a deeper knowledge and wider experience, such judgment is found to be erroneous. The dishonest man may have some admirable virtues which the other does not possess; and the honest man obnoxious vices which are absent in the other. The honest man reaps the good results of his honest thoughts and acts; he also brings upon himself the sufferings which his vices produce. The dishonest man likewise garners his own suffering and happiness.

It is pleasing to human vanity to believe that one suffers because of one's virtue; but not until a man has extirpated every sickly, bitter, and impure thought from his soul, can he be in a position to know and declare that his sufferings are the result of his good, and not of his bad qualities; and on the way to, yet long before he has reached that supreme perfection, he will have found, working in his mind and life, the great law which is absolutely just, and which cannot, therefore, give good for evil, evil for good.

Possessed of such knowledge, he will then know, looking back upon his past ignorance and blindness, that his life is, and always was, justly ordered, and that all his past experiences, good and bad, were the equitable outworking of his evolving, yet unevolved self.

<u>The Work</u>:

This principle takes 5 minutes to learn and a lifetime to master. We all have deep habits and patterns that are counter to our true desire. When we face and confront them it stirs up feelings that may be intense and unexpected, we often seek to avoid those feelings. Only by facing those feelings do we become the Hero's and Heroine's of our lives and go on the adventure to become what we choose.

Be patient.

Good thoughts and actions can never produce bad results; bad thoughts and actions can never produce good results. This is but saying that nothing can come from corn but corn, nothing from nettles but nettles. Men understand this law in the natural world, and work with it; but few understand it in the mental and moral world (though its operation there is just as simple and undeviating), and they, therefore, do not cooperate with it.

Suffering is always the effect of wrong thought in some direction. It is an indication that the individual is out of harmony with himself, with the law of his being. The sole and supreme use of suffering is to purify, to burn out all that is useless and impure. Suffering ceases for him who is pure. There could be no object in burning gold after the dross had been removed, and a perfectly pure and enlightened being could not suffer.

The circumstances which a man encounters with suffering are the result of his own mental inharmony. The circumstances which a man encounters with blessedness are the result of his own mental harmony. Blessedness, not material possessions, is the measure of right thought; wretchedness, not lack of material possessions, is the measure of wrong thought. A man may be cursed and rich; he may be blessed and poor. Blessedness and riches are only joined together when the riches are rightly and wisely used. And the poor man only descends into wretchedness when he regards his lot as a burden unjustly imposed.

> <u>Contemplation</u>:
>
> Money will never buy you happiness, though it will alleviate some stresses. Being poor doesn't demand unhappiness, it's all a matter of your level of gratitude and the connections you feel in life.

Indigence and indulgence are the two extremes of wretchedness. They are both equally unnatural and the result of mental disorder.

A man is not rightly conditioned until he is a happy, healthy, and prosperous being; and happiness, health, and prosperity are the result of a harmonious adjustment of the inner with the outer of the man with his surroundings.

A man only begins to be a man when he ceases to whine and revile, and commences to search for the hidden justice which regulates his life. And he adapts his mind to that regulating factor, he ceases to accuse others as the cause of his condition, and builds himself up in strong and noble thoughts; ceases to kick against circumstances, but begins to use them as aids to his more rapid progress, and as a means of discovering the hidden powers and possibilities within himself.

Law, not confusion, is the dominating principle in the universe; justice, not injustice, is the soul and substance of life. Righteousness, not corruption, is the molding and moving force in the spiritual government of the world. This being so, man has but to right himself to find that the universe is right. And during the process of putting himself right, he will find that as he alters his thoughts towards things and other people, things and other people will alter towards him.

The proof of this truth is in every person, and it therefore admits of easy investigation by systematic introspection and self-analysis. Let a man radically alter his thoughts, and he will be astonished at the rapid transformation it will effect in the material conditions of his life. Men imagine that thought can be kept secret, but it cannot. It rapidly crystallizes into habit, and habit solidifies into circumstance. Bestial thoughts crystallize into habits of drunkenness and sensuality, which solidify into circumstances of destitution and disease. Impure thoughts of every kind crystallize into enervating and confusing habits, which solidify into distracting and adverse circumstances. Thoughts of fear, doubt, and indecision crystallize into weak, unmanly, and irresolute habits, which solidify into circumstances of failure, indigence, and slavish dependence.

Lazy thoughts crystallize into weak, habits of uncleanliness and dishonesty, which solidify into circumstances of foulness and beggary. Hateful and condemnatory thoughts crystallize into habits of accusation and violence, which solidify into circumstances of injury and persecution. Selfish thoughts of all kinds crystallize into habits of self-seeking, which solidify into distressful circumstances.

On the other hand, beautiful thoughts of all kinds crystallize into habits of grace and kindliness, which solidify into genial and sunny circumstances. Pure thoughts crystallize into habits of temperance and self-control, which solidify into circumstances of repose and peace. Thoughts of courage, self-reliance, and decision crystallize into manly habits, which solidify into circumstances of success, plenty, and freedom. Energetic thoughts crystallize into habits of cleanliness and industry, which solidify into circumstances of pleasantness. Gentle and forgiving thoughts crystallize into habits of gentleness, which solidify into protective and preservative circumstances. Loving and unselfish thoughts which solidify into circumstances of sure and abiding prosperity and true riches.

> Question:
> So, the question you need to be asking yourself is "how can I adjust my life so I feel good and have better, clearer, happier thoughts?"

A particular train of thought persisted in, be it good or bad, cannot fail to produce its results on the character and circumstances. A man cannot directly choose his circumstances, but he can choose his thoughts, and so indirectly, yet surely, shape his circumstances.

Nature helps every man to gratification of the thoughts

which he most encourages, and opportunities are presented which will most speedily bring to the surface both the good and the evil thoughts.

> The Work:
> Examine your present, it is a reflection of your past. Decide what to keep and what to change

Let a man cease from his sinful thoughts, and all the world will soften towards him, and be ready to help him. Let him put away his weakly and sickly thoughts, and the opportunities will spring up on every hand to aid his strong resolves. Let him encourage good thoughts, and no hard fate shall bind him down to wretchedness and shame. The world is your kaleidoscope, and the varying combinations of colors which at every succeeding moment it presents to you are the exquisitely adjusted pictures of your ever-moving thoughts.

You will be what you will to be;

Let failure find its false content In that poor word, "environment," But spirit scorns it, and is free.

It masters time, it conquers space; It cows that boastful trickster, Chance, And bids the tyrant Circumstance Uncrown, and fill a servant's place.

The human Will, that force unseen, The offspring of deathless Soul, Can hew a way to any goal, Though walls of granite intervene.

Be not impatient in delay, But wait as one who understands; When spirit rises and commands, The gods are ready to obey.

<u>Exercise</u>:

What are some major areas in life where I created change intentionally?

What did I "sacrifice" to make it happen? Looking back was it worth the sacrifice?

_____
_____
_____
_____
_____
_____
_____
_____
_____
_____
_____
_____
_____
_____
_____
_____
_____
_____
_____
_____

Effects Of Thoughts On Health And Body

The body is the servant of the mind. It obeys the operations of the mind, whether they be deliberately chosen or automatically expressed. At the bidding of unlawful thoughts the body sinks rapidly into disease and decay; at the command of glad and beautiful thoughts it becomes clothed with youthfulness and beauty.

Contemplation:

We have all seen someone age 60 who looks 40 and someone 40 who looks 60! Genetics plays a small role, it's also the thoughts and actions one takes to create and maintain a healthy and youthful attitude and physique.

Disease and health, like circumstances, are rooted in thought. Sickly thoughts will express themselves through a sickly body. Thoughts of fear have been known to kill a man as speedily as a bullet and they are continually killing thousands of people just as surely though less rapidly. The people who live in fear of disease are the people who get it. Anxiety quickly demoralizes the whole body, and lays it open to the entrance of disease; while impure thoughts, even if not physically indulged, will sooner shatter the nervous system.

Reflection:

I remember a story from some years ago about a fraternity initiation. They had all the new fraternity brothers there for the induction ceremony. They informed them that they would all be branded with a hot iron. They then blindfolded them all and came and touched their skin with ice cubes. One of the young men actually had a heart attack

> and died from the shock of the ice cube he thought was a red hot brand.
>
> It was a very sad story, and it really shows the power of the mind on the body. The two are intricately connected and always influencing each other back and forth.

Strong pure, and happy thoughts build up the body in vigor and grace. The body is a delicate and plastic instrument, which responds readily to the thoughts by which it is impressed, and habits of thought will produce their own effects, good or bad, upon it.

Men will continue to have impure and poisoned blood, so long as they propagate unclean thoughts. Out of a clean heart comes a clean life and a clean body. Out of a defiled mind proceeds a defiled life and a corrupt body. Thought is the fount of action, life and manifestation; make the fountain pure, and all will be pure.

Change of diet will not help a man who will not change his thoughts. When a man makes his thoughts pure, he no longer desires impure food.

> <u>The Work</u>:
> When you do both at the same time you achieve exponential results. (hint,hint)

Clean thoughts make clean habits. The so-called saint who does not wash his body is not a saint. He who has strengthened and purified his thoughts does not need to consider the malevolent. If you would perfect your body, guard your mind. If you would renew your body, beautify your mind. Thoughts of malice, envy, and disappointment, despondency, rob the body of its health and grace. A sour face does not come by chance; it is made by sour thoughts. Wrinkles that mar are drawn by folly, passion, pride.

I know a woman of ninety-six who has the bright, innocent face of a girl. I know a man well under middle age whose face is drawn into in harmonious contours. The one is the result of a sweet and sunny disposition; the other is the outcome of passion and discontent.

As you cannot have a sweet and wholesome abode unless you admit the air and sunshine freely into your rooms, so a strong body and a bright, happy, or serene countenance can only result from the free admittance into the mind of thoughts of joy and goodwill and serenity.

> ### The Work:
>
> Your mind often follows your physiology, if you're having a hard time with your thoughts then simply change how you're holding yourself physically. Stand tall, put your shoulders back and smile. It's hard to feel bad for long when you hold yourself up like this.
>
> Studies have been shows than if depressed people smile in front of a mirror for 10 minutes a day for 30 days they feel remarkably better! Many even say that their depression is completely gone!
>
> They created a new internal vision of themselves as a happy smiling person and the mind responded by creating more happy hormones and the snowball effect kept it going.

On the faces of the aged there are wrinkles made by sympathy others by strong and pure thought, and others are carved by passion; who cannot distinguish them? With those who have lived righteously, age is calm, peaceful, and softly mellowed, like the setting sun.

I have recently seen a philosopher on his death-bed. He was not old except in years. He died as sweetly and peacefully as he had lived.

There is no physician like cheerful thought for dissipating the ills of the body; there is no comforter to compare with goodwill for dispersing the shadows of grief and sorrow. To live continually in thoughts of ill-will, cynicism, suspicion, and envy, is to be confined in a self-made prison hole. But to think well of all, to be cheerful with all, to patiently learn to find the good in all--such unselfish thoughts are the very portals of heaven; and to dwell day by day in thoughts of peace toward every creature will bring abounding peace to their possessor.

Exercises:

What am I like at my most healthy?

What kind of thoughts are regularly in my head?

What else in my life contributes to me being healthy?

___
___
___
___
___
___
___
___
___
___
___
___
___
___
___
___
___
___
___
___

_____
_____
_____
_____

What are the top 10 things I can do to increase my feeling of well being. Things that are easily accessible and can be done to increase my happiness and positivity.

1._____

2._____

3._____

4._____

5._____

6._____

7._____

8._____

9._____

10._____

> How can I create a weekly schedule to include all these 10 things?

Thought And Purpose

Until thought is linked with purpose there is no intelligent accomplishment. With the majority the bark of thought is allowed to "drift" upon the ocean of life. Aimlessness is a vice, and such drifting must not continue for him who would steer clear of catastrophe and destruction.

They who have no central purpose in their life fall an easy prey to petty worries, fears, troubles, and self-pitying, all of which are indications of weakness, which lead, just as surely as deliberately planned sins (though by a diff route), to failure, unhappiness, and loss, for weakness cannot persist in a power-evolving universe.

A man should conceive of a legitimate purpose in his heart, and set out to accomplish it. He should make this purpose the centralizing point of his thoughts. It may take the form of a spiritual ideal, or it may be a worldly object, according to his nature at the time being. Whichever it is, he should steadily focus his thought-forces upon the object he had set before him. He should make this purpose his supreme duty and should devote himself to its attainment, not allowing his thoughts to wander away into ephemeral fancies, longings, and imaginings. This is the royal road to self-control and true concentration of thought. Even if he fails again and again to accomplish his purpose--as he must until weakness is overcome--the strength of character gained will be the measure of his true success, and this will form a new starting point for future power and triumph.

> **Reflection:**
>
> There is a common belief that if you focus on a bunch of things at the same time one will eventually work out.
>
> People look at the famous entrepreneurs of the day and see all their endeavors and say "Well if they became wealthy doing all those things then that's the model for success".
>
> What you need to realize is that starting out all successful people focused on building one thing until it was wildly successful and could be automated or run by someone else. Only then did they shift focus to another single endeavor.

Those who are not prepared for the apprehension of a great purpose, should fix the thoughts upon the faultless performance of their duty, no matter how insignificant their task may appear. Only in this way can the thoughts be gathered and focused, and resolution and energy be developed. Once this is done, there is nothing which may not be accomplished.

The weakest soul knowing its own weakness, and believing this truth--that strength can only be developed by effort and practice--will, thus believing, at once begin to exert itself. And, adding effort to effort, patience to patience, and strength to strength, will never cease to develop and will at last grow divinely strong.

As the physically weak man can make himself strong by careful and patient training, so the man of weak thoughts can make them strong by exercising himself in right thinking.

To put away aimlessness and weakness and to begin to think with purpose is to enter the ranks of those strong ones who only recognize failure as one of the pathways to attainment. Who make all conditions serve them, and who think strongly, attempt fearlessly, and accomplish masterfully

Having conceived of his purpose, a man should mentally mark out a straight pathway to its achievement, looking neither to the right nor left. Doubts and fears should be rigorously excluded.

They are disintegrating elements which break up the straight line of effort, rendering it crooked, ineffectual, useless. Thoughts of doubt and fear can never accomplish anything. They always lead to failure. Purpose, energy, power to do, and all strong thoughts cease when doubt and fear creep in.

> Contemplation:
>
> While having this straight vision remember that the journey itself is never straight there will always be things that push you off course, just like a boat sailing across the ocean.
>
> Your job is simply to keep the focus and redirect your efforts towards the goal as various things come up and distract you or lead you off course.

The will to do springs from the knowledge that we can do. Doubt and fear are the great enemies of knowledge, and he who encourages them, who does not slay them, thwarts himself at every step.

He who has conquered doubt and fear has conquered failure. His every thought is allied with power, and all difficulties are bravely met and overcome. His purposes are seasonably planted, and they bloom and bring forth fruit that does not fall prematurely to the ground.

Thought allied fearlessly to purpose becomes creative force. He who knows this is ready to become something higher and stronger than a bundle of wavering thoughts and fluctuating sensations. He who does this has become the conscious and intelligent wielder of his mental powers.

Exercises:

What is my absolute #1 focus right now?
_____
_____
_____
_____
_____
_____

Why is this a MUST for me in life?

If I don't have the specific answer, respond with the general idea of what I want or how I want to feel.
_____
_____
_____
_____
_____
_____
_____
_____
_____

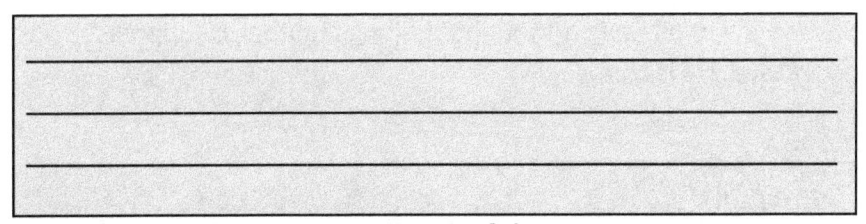

The Thought-Factor In Achievement

All that a man achieves and all that he fails to achieve is the direct result of his own thoughts. In a justly ordered universe, where loss of equipoise would mean total destruction, individual responsibility must be absolute. A man's weakness and strength, purity and impurity, are his own and not another man's. They are brought about by himself and not by another; and they can only be altered by himself, never by another. His condition is also his own, and not another man's. His sufferings and his happiness are evolved from within. As he thinks, so is he; as he continues to think, so he remains.

A strong man cannot help a weaker unless that weaker is willing to be helped. And even then the weak man must become strong of himself. He must, by his own efforts, develop the strength which he admires in another. None but himself can alter his condition.

It has been usual for men to think and to say, "Many men are slaves because one is an oppressor; let us hate the oppressor!" But there is amongst an increasing few a tendency to reverse this judgment and to say, "One man is an oppressor because many are slaves; let us despise the slaves."

The truth is that oppressor and slaves are cooperators in ignorance, and, while seeming to afflict each other, are in reality, afflicting themselves. A perfect knowledge perceives the action of law in the weakness of the oppressed and the misapplied power of the oppressor. A perfect love, seeing the suffering which both states entail, condemns neither; a perfect compassion embraces both oppressor and oppressed. He who has conquered weakness and has pushed away all selfish thoughts belongs neither to oppressor nor oppressed. He is free.

> **Contemplation:**
>
> There is often an US vs THEM feeling that people have. The rich, the 1%, the powerful elite are often seen by people as holding them back and preventing them from moving forward in life.
>
> We have often a sense of "false freedom" in America, we have more money and stuff than other cultures, yet 35% of people live paycheck to paycheck. More than half don't have enough savings to last 6 months. And for 99%, if you left your job tomorrow the income would stop! That may not seem like slavery, but it certainly isn't freedom.

A man can only rise, conquer, and achieve by lifting up his thoughts. He can only remain weak, abject, and miserably by refusing to lift up his thoughts.

Before a man can achieve anything, even in worldly things, he must lift his thoughts above slavish animal indulgence. He may not, in order to succeed, give up all animality and selfishness, necessarily, but a portion of it must, at least, be sacrificed. A man whose first thought is bestial indulgence could neither think clearly nor plan methodically. He could not find and develop his latent resources and would fail in any undertaking. Not having begun to manfully control his thoughts, he is not in a position to control affairs and to adopt serious responsibilities. He is not fit to act independently and stand alone. But he is limited only by the thoughts that he chooses.

There can be no progress nor achievement without sacrifice, and a man's worldly success will be by the measure that he sacrifices his confused animal thoughts, and fixes his mind on the development of his plans, and the strengthening of his resolution and self-reliance. The higher he lifts his thoughts, the greater will be his success, the more blessed and enduring will be his achievements.

The universe does not favor the greedy, the dishonest, the vicious, although on the mere surface it sometimes may appear to do so. It helps the honest, the magnanimous, the virtuous. All the great teachers of the ages have declared this in varying ways, and to prove it and to know it a man has but to persist in making himself increasingly virtuous by lifting his thoughts.

Intellectual achievements are the result of thought consecrated to the search for knowledge or for the beautiful and true in nature. Such achievements may sometimes be connected with vanity and ambition, but they are not the outcome of those characteristics. They are the natural outgrowth of long and arduous effort, and of pure and unselfish thoughts.

Spiritual achievements are the consummation of holy aspirations. He who lives constantly in the conception of noble and lofty thoughts, who dwells upon all that is pure and selfless, will, as surely as the sun reaches its zenith and the moon its full, become wise and noble in character and rise into a position of influence and blessedness. Achievement of any kind is the crown of effort, the diadem of thought. By the aid of self-control, resolution, purity, righteousness, and well-directed thought a man ascends. By the aid of animality, indolence, impurity, corruption, and confusion of thought a man descends.

Meditation:

Think of it this way , the only difference between you and the person who is wildly successful is the size of your dream and time. As long as you cultivate a large, powerful vision for your life and keep the focus for long enough you will get there.

A man may rise to high success in the world, even to lofty attitudes in the spiritual realm, and again descend into weakness and wretchedness by allowing arrogant, selfish, and corrupt thoughts to take possession of him.

Victories attained by right thought can be maintained only by watchfulness. Many give way when success is assured, and rapidly fall back into failure.

All achievements, whether in the business, intellectual, or spiritual world, are the result of definitely directed thought. They are governed by the same law, and are of the same method. The only difference lies in the object of attainment.

He who would accomplish little need sacrifice little; he who would achieve much must sacrifice much. He who would attain highly must sacrifice greatly.

Exercises:

What are the things I do instead of focusing on my true dreams in life?

_____
_____
_____
_____
_____
_____
_____
_____
_____

What am I willing to sacrifice or give up in life to get where I want to go?

_____
_____
_____
_____
_____
_____

What is the limitation I have placed on myself in terms of what I am able to accomplish in life?

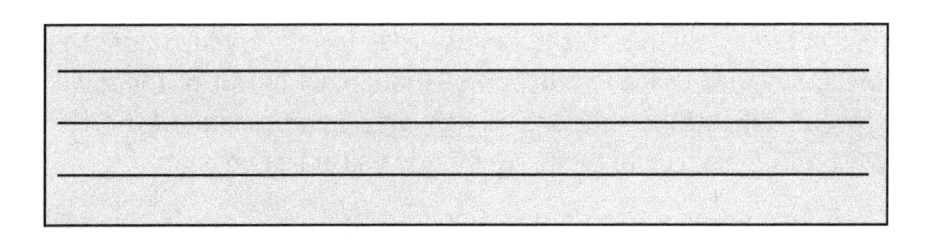

Visions And Ideals

The dreamers are the saviors of the world. As the visible world is sustained by the invisible, so men, through all their trials and sins and sordid vocations, are nourished by the beautiful visions of their solitary dreamers. Humanity cannot forget its dreamers; it cannot let their ideals fade and die; it lives in them; it knows them as the realities which it shall one day see and know.

Composer, sculptor, painter, poet, prophet, sage--these are the makers of the after-world, the architects of heaven. The world is beautiful because they have lived. Without them, laboring humanity would perish.

Reflection:
Today it's the musicians, the filmmakers, the inventors, the technology guru's, political and religious icons who are shaping the minds of the world. We all have the option to shape the future of our lives and the lives of future generations.

He who cherishes a beautiful vision, a lofty ideal in his heart, will one day realize it. Columbus cherished a vision of another world and he discovered it. Copernicus fostered the vision of a multiplicity of worlds and a wider universe, and he revealed it. Buddha beheld the vision of a spiritual world of stainless beauty and perfect peace, and he entered into it.

Cherish your visions; cherish your ideals. Cherish the music that stirs in your heart, the beauty that forms in your mind, the loveliness that drapes your purest thoughts. For out of them will grow all delightful conditions, all heavenly environment; of these, if you but remain true to them, your world will at last be built.

To desire is to obtain; to aspire is to achieve. Shall man's basest desires receive the fullest measure of gratification, and his purest aspirations starve for lack of sustenance? Such is not the Law. Such a condition can never obtain, "Ask and receive."

Dream lofty dreams, and as you dream, so shall you become. Your vision is the promise of what you shall one day be; your ideal is the prophecy of what you shall at last unveil.

> Meditation:
>
> Dream lofty dreams, and as you dream, so shall you become. Your vision is the promise of what you shall one day be; your ideal is the prophecy of what you shall at last unveil.

The greatest achievement was at first and for a time a dream. The oak sleeps in the acorn; the bird waits in the egg. And in the highest vision of a soul a waking angel stirs. Dreams are the seedlings of realities.

Your circumstances may be uncongenial, but they shall not remain so if you only perceive an ideal and strive to reach it. You cannot travel within and stand still without. Here is a youth hard pressed by poverty and labor. Confined long hours in an unhealthy workshop; unschooled and lacking all the arts of refinement. But he dreams of better things. He thinks of intelligence, or refinement, of grace and beauty. He conceives of, mentally builds up, an ideal condition of life. The wider liberty and a larger scope takes possession of him; unrest urges him to action, and he uses all his spare times and means to the development of his latent powers and resources. Very soon so altered has his mind become that the workshop can no longer hold him. It has become so out of harmony with his mind-set that it falls out of his life as a garment is cast aside. And with the growth of opportunities that fit the scope of his expanding powers, he passes out of it altogether.

Years later we see this youth as a grown man. We find him a master of certain forces of the mind that he wields with worldwide influence and almost unequaled power. In his hands he holds the cords of gigantic responsibilities; he speaks and lives are changed; men and women hang upon his words and remold their characters. Sun-like, he becomes the fixed and luminous center around which innumerable destinies revolve.

> The Work:
>
> Your present situation means nothing in terms of your potential, pay it no mind. Now of course, you need to handle things in the present to set yourself up for the future, just remember there are things coming that you cannot possibly conceive of right now.
>
> You can stay exactly where you are or you can decide to go somewhere different, the choice is yours.

He has realized the vision of his youth. He has become one with his ideal.

And you, too, will realize the vision (not just the idle wish) of your heart, be it base or beautiful, or a mixture of both; for you will always gravitate toward that which you secretly love most. Into your hands will be placed the exact results of your own thoughts. You will receive that which you earn; no more, no less. Whatever your present environment may be, you will fall, remain, or rise with your thoughts--your vision, your ideal. You will become as small as your controlling desire, as great as your dominant aspiration.

The thoughtless, the ignorant, and the indolent, seeing only the apparent effects of things and not the things themselves, talk of luck, of fortune, and chance. Seeing a man grow rich, they say, "How lucky he is!"

Observing another become skilled intellectually, they exclaim, "How highly favored he is!" And noting the saintly character and wide influence of another, they remark, "How chance helps him at every turn!" They do not see the trials and failures and struggles which these men have encountered in order to gain their experience. They have no knowledge of the sacrifices they have made, of the undaunted efforts they have put forth, of the faith they have exercised so that they might overcome the apparently insurmountable and realize the vision of their heart. They do not know the darkness and the heartaches; they only see the light and joy, and call it "luck." Do not see the long, arduous journey, but only behold the pleasant goal and call it "good fortune." Do not understand the process, but only perceive the result, and call it "chance."

In all human affairs there are efforts, and there are results. The strength of the effort is the measure of the result. Change is not. Gifts, powers, material, intellectual, and spiritual possessions are the fruits of effort. They are thoughts completed, objectives accomplished, visions realized.

The vision that you glorify in your mind, the ideal that you enthrone in your heart -- this you will build your life by; this you will become.

The Work:

We all have certain things that come more naturally to us. We also have things that we enjoy more so than the next person. If you are 5'6" it doesn't make sense to focus all your effort to be a professional basketball player, now with practice you can get better, better than most people, but there is a certain limitation there. It's important to find what you're naturally good at and what you naturally enjoy. When you find this work becomes play and play creates success and abundance.

This comes very quickly to some people, for others it takes more time and experimentation. Life is a buffet, sometimes you need to sample a lot of dishes to find one you love the taste of! Find a way to enjoy the process of exploring, have some pre-set parameters to indicate if you should stop or continue.

Follow your gut, your gut is never wrong. Develop a way to determine the difference between your gut instinct and your ego.

Don't waste time going after something you know isn't right, stop, readjust and move in a new direction.

Exercise:

Considering that the size of my dream is important, what does my dream look like when I multiply it by 10?

_____
_____
_____
_____
_____
_____
_____

How can I engage in my vision in a way that uses my natural talents and the things I naturally enjoy?

_____
_____
_____
_____
_____
_____
_____
_____
_____
_____
_____

Serenity

Calmness of mind is one of the beautiful jewels of wisdom. It is the result of long and patient effort in self-control. Its presence is an indication of ripened experience, and of a more than ordinary knowledge of the laws and operations of thought.

A man becomes calm in the measure that he understands himself as a thought-evolved being. For such knowledge necessitates the understanding of others as the result of thought, and as he develops a right understanding, and sees ever more clearly the internal relations of things by the action of cause and effect, he ceases to fuss, fume, worry, and grieve. He remains poised, steadfast, serene.

The calm man, having learned how to govern himself, knows how to adapt himself to others. And they, in turn reverence his spiritual strength. They feel that they can learn from him and rely upon him. The more tranquil a man becomes, the greater is his success, his influence, his power for good. Even the ordinary trader will find his business prosperity increase as he develops a greater self-control and equanimity, for people will always prefer to deal with a man whose demeanor is equitable.

The strong, calm man is always loved and revered. He is like a shade-giving tree in a thirsty land, or a sheltering rock in a storm. Who does not love a tranquil heart, a sweet-tempered, balanced life? It does not matter whether it rains or shines, or what changes come to those who possess these blessings, for they are always serene and calm. That exquisite poise of character that we call serenity is the last lesson of culture. It is the flowering of life, the fruitage of the soul. It is precious as wisdom--more desirable than fine gold. How insignificant mere money-seeking looks in comparison with a serene life. A life that dwells in the ocean of truth, beneath the waves, beyond the reach of the tempests, in the Eternal Calm!

> Contemplation:
> Who do you know in your life that exudes a sense of calmness and serenity whenever you see them?

How many people we know who sour their lives, who ruin all that is sweet and beautiful by explosive tempers, who destroy their poise of character and make bad blood! It is a question whether the great majority of people do not ruin their lives and mar their happiness by lack of self-control. How few people we meet in life who are well balanced, who have that exquisite poise which is characteristic of the finished character!

Yes, humanity surges with uncontrolled passion, is tumultuous with ungoverned grief, is blown about by anxiety and doubt. Only the wise man, only he whose thoughts are controlled and purified, makes the winds and the storms of the soul obey him. Tempest-tossed souls, wherever you may be, under whatever conditions you may live, know this: In the ocean of life the isles of blessedness are smiling and the sunny shore of your ideal awaits your coming. Keep your hands firmly upon the helm of thought. In the core of your soul reclines the commanding Master; He does but sleep; wake Him. Self-control is strength. Right thought is mastery. Calmness is power. Say unto your heart, "Peace. Be still!"

Exercises:

What influences in life tend to push me out of that state of deep calm and serenity?

What am I grateful for?

What thoughts am I going to work to keep in the front of my mind from this point on?

How can I remind myself to keep that focus when I am challenged?

What was my biggest takeaway from this book?

What can I do on a regular basis to feel good?

_____
_____
_____
_____
_____
_____

What helps me become centered and think more clearly and positively?

_____
_____
_____
_____
_____
_____

How can I arrange life to get MORE of that?

_____
_____
_____
_____
_____

CPSIA information can be obtained
at www.ICGtesting.com
Printed in the USA
BVHW041337010519
547057BV00029B/1793/P